I Remember:
Creative Writing of Indianapolis Youth

INwords

I Remember: Creative Writing of Indianapolis Youth

Edited by Darolyn "Lyn" Jones, Mark Latta, Barbara Shoup, Julianna Thibodeaux, Shari Wagner, Michael Baumann, James Figy, and Caroline Wilson

Published by INwords

ISBN: 978-0-9849501-9-5

I Remember:

Creative Writing of Indianapolis Youth

Edited by

Darolyn "Lyn" Jones, Mark Latta, Barbara Shoup, Julianna Thibodeaux, and Shari Wagner

INwords

P.O. Box 30407
Indianapolis, IN 46230-0407

Be a Writer.
The Writers' Center of Indiana

Summer Youth Program Fund

hff

The INDIANAPOLIS FOUNDATION
A CICF Affiliate
inspiring philanthropy

LILLY ENDOWMENT
+ I N C +

Table of Contents

The Writers' Center of Indiana is pleased to present this collection of student writing from the 2012 "Building a Rainbow" Program. We had only a few hours a week over a four week period to work with these young writers, so we are especially proud of the strong pieces found here. And while we serve a distinct student population at each site, we value the collective and unified voice of the youth who represent our urban community.

This year, we had the honor of partnering with three diverse program sites that bring summer programing to students in the greater Indianapolis area, including Saint Florian Center's Youth Leadership Camp, La Plaza's Leadership Institute for Latino Youth (LILY), and Concord Neighborhood Center's Summer Day Camp.

Writers' Center instructors, university student interns, and volunteers bring writing expertise to the program, as well as an enthusiastic and personal teaching style. Special thanks to instructors and editors Darolyn "Lyn" Jones, Mark Latta, Barbara Shoup, Julianna Thibodeaux, and Shari Wagner; student editors Michael Baumann, James Figy, and Caroline Wilson; student interns Amy Demien, Corrie Herron, Brett Hiatt, Zhen Zhen Liu, Vienna Wagner, and Jessica Tatum; and our regular volunteers

Brandon Bloom, Patricia Cupp, and Carol Weiss.

Many thanks to the Summer Youth Program Fund (SYPF) of Indianapolis; Executive Director of the Writers' Center of Indiana, Barbara Shoup; the Board of Directors and staff of the Writers' Center; Summer Program Director of the Writers' Center, Darolyn "Lyn" Jones; Saint Florian Center Executive Director, Tony Williamson; Saint Florian Center Program Director Michael Morgan; LaPlaza Executive Director Miriam Acevedo Davis; LaPlaza Education Director, Jasmine Roberts; Concord Neighborhood Center Executive Director, Niki Girls; Concord Neighborhood Center Summer Day Camp Program Director, Now for the Future Program Director, Paula J. Richter-Hayes.

Finally, and most importantly, thanks to the young writers in this book who trusted us enough to share their voices. We will always remember you.

To learn more about the Writers' Center of Indiana and our youth "Building a Rainbow" Memoir Program, please visit www.indianawriters.org. To learn more about the Summer Program Youth Fund (SYPF), visit: http://www.summeryouthprogramfund-indy.org/
Saint Florian Center, visit: http://www.saintfloriancenter.org/
La Plaza, visit: http://www.laplaza-indy.org/
Concord Neighborhood Center, visit: http://concordindy.org/.

***

One of my favorite things in the whole world is to stand in the middle of a classroom surrounded by children with their heads bent, writing furiously, no sound but the scratch of pencils on the page. Another one of my favorite things is to listen to them read their stories aloud. I love how proud—and often a little surprised—they are at having written so well.

No wonder I look forward to to the Writers' Center of Indiana's "Building a Rainbow" program every year.

Funded by the Summer Youth Program Fund (SYPF), the "Building a Rainbow" serves a diverse group of young people in Indianapolis, improving their writing and literacy skills through a series of creative writing exercises that teach them how to write the stories of their own lives. The program is named after a colorful, whimsical poster of a half-made rainbow that is covered with tiny stick figures painting, hammering, and operating cranes and trucks as they work to finish it. The image is a visual reminder that there are many small steps in creating something beautiful—a piece of writing, a dream, a goal, a life.

Working one-on-one, Writers' Center instructors, student interns, and volunteers help the young writers get their words on the page and also encourage them to reflect upon the experiences they've written about, considering how what they've learned can help them make their dreams come true.

A third—maybe, the best of all—favorite thing is to be able to put a book in the hands of a young writer and watch his face light up as he opens it to find his own work inside.

This book, *I Remember: Creative Writing of Indianapolis Youth*, is bursting with lively writing from students attending the St. Florian Leadership Camp, La Plaza's Leadership Insititute for Latino Youth (LILY), and the Concord Neighborhood Center Summer Day Camp. Their stories will take you from a chair in a beauty shop to a beach in Mexico; from Grandma's kitchen to the Taj Mahal. You'll plunge downward in a rollercoaster, paddle a canoe up a creek, and join in a Puerto Rican folk dance with them. You'll meet the people they love.

Above all, you'll hear their voices: glorious young voices full of hope for the future.

Listen! Enjoy!

Barbara Shoup
Executive Director
Writers' Center of Indiana

Founded by Indianapolis Firefighters in 1992, the Saint Florian Center provides Indianapolis youth an opportunity to develop leadership skills, problem solving methods, and survival tactics, as well as fostering core values, such as honesty, respect, responsibility, and character. After school programs, tobacco free programs, rites of passage programs, alcohol and violence prevention programs, college preparation programs, and youth ambassador programs are among the services the Saint Florian Center provides for young people.

The Saint Florian Center Youth Development Camp, which serves approximately 100 students each summer, age 6-18, has been in operation for twenty years. Over the course of seven weeks, students learn about the world around them and how to be successful in it by participating in a wide range of activities that include academics, science and technology, team building, physical fitness, and art. This year, Core and Junior Cadets improved their writing skills by writing the stories of their own lives; some took part in a spoken word workshop with poet, Erin Livingstone. In 2011, Time Magazine featured the Saint Florian Center Youth Development Camp as an extraordinary summer learning program.

Lyn Jones, Julianna Thibodeaux,
and Barb Shoup

Ahlena S.

I am From the Wii and Racecars

I am from the Wii and racecars.
I am from playing outside with my best friend.
I am from the playground.
I am from the Disney Channel.

Alexis P.

I Remember My Time in Texas

In Texas, I remember when we first had to all four sit in the back seats. It was NOT comfortable. Then other times we had to do it were not bad. It was okay. One time, my brother sat on the floor, and it was comfortable. But I still don't want to go back.

King's Island

At King's Island first we have to go through the entrance. Then after we pay we get to get in and do anything. First we walk around and see what's there. The thing I like best at King's Island is the Diamondback. It has the face of a dragon, then the seats, and the dragon's tail in back. I get on with my dad. We sit together. My sister and my auntie sit together. First they put their thumbs up to say "All clear." We go up the hill really slow, then down really fast. I'm scared. We went past water and it splashed. We went all the way back to where we were. They said did you enjoy yourself, and everyone said "Yes" real loud.

Allen J.

I Remember...
I remember my first baseball game.
I remember the day I got glass in my arm.
I remember the soccer game I watched.
I remember going to St. Petersburg, Florida.
I remember playing my first basketball game.
I remember coming to my first day of camp.
I remember playing my Playstation for the first time.
I remember eating Thanksgiving dinner
I remember eating fried dumplins for the first time.
I remember eating cod fish, and I
I remember eating chocolate ice cream for the first time.
I remember kindergarten graduation.
I remember a recent sleepover at her house.

I Picked the Bigger
I was choosing a bat to hit with. I saw a 31 inch and a 30 inch bat. I picked the bigger. I was sitting in the dugout and Coach called me to tell me I was up to bat. I chose a bat and went to the batter's box. Strike one, strike two, after hearing and seeing two strikes fly past me. I took the bat off my shoulder and then I heard *bing*. I hit the ball hit the bat and I ran to first base.

Amari S.
The First Day was Mostly Just Instructions
I remember my grandma dying.
I remember being a straight A student.
I remember my favorite teacher Mrs. Reid.
I remember my first year of camp.
I remember cleaning 2 horses' hooves.
Black crinkly and soft horse hair—
Tail was amazing.
Rocket.
Water in a bucket, warm.
Scrubbed hard so all the crud would come off
muddy hoof.

Grandma Nadia
I remember her long hair.
I remember her grey hair.
I remember her long nails.
I remember her nails were so long they were
curly nails.
I remember mom's voice.
I remember she is tall.
I remember she calls me sweetie.
I remember moo moo.
I remember she looks like my mom.
I remember her oxygen machine on her side.
I remember she walks pretty much like my
mom.
I remember the sound of her voice.
I remember she splits things equally.
I remember her hugs.
I remember her kisses and love.

I remember she was calm, pleasant, carrying, loving and understanding.
She tells really funny jokes. I remember she would say it's okay, you can work through it, keep trying. I remember her being proud of me. I remember she told me that I was allergic to pineapple juice, but it was true. I remember her saying don't say hate. I remember her saying pickle juice helps you grow. I remember her birthday is on Christmas. I remember an ornament with her picture in the middle of it. The ornament is gold and red.

My Classroom
Brown and white
Her hair was natural
Her name is Keanna Reid
She's engaged
White board not a chalkboard
Wooden desk
Black and brown
Suits
Skirts
Flats
Like to go to the nails shop
You have to shake the nails
Tan crinkly walls
Elmo
Square desks

Amaya F.

Scar

My Dad is a firefighter who was in a fire and got lung cancer. I was 2 years old and one day he had to go to the hospital. My mom, my sister, and I went to see him in the hospital. We all said goodbye and we love him. The surgery lasted an hour. I cried and said, "I don't want my dad to die." I remember after the surgery my dad had a big scar on his back because they cut half of his left lung. I remember he spent several weeks in the hospital. Finally he could come home. He went to a firefighter care center every day. They helped him get stronger. After resting for a month at home he went back to work but was still in training to see if he got stronger. Today he fights fires and still does his job.

Amiia G.

Mommy

I remember yesterday was mommy's
birthday. She's 31.
I remember my mommy is a good teacher.
I remember my mommy and I were sad when
grandpa died.
I remember when my mommy surprised me
on my birthday.
I remember when my mommy and I went to
visit daddy and we would eat lunch on
Fridays or Saturdays.

I remember when it was my YaYa's birthday. My mommy and I gave him balloons and four flowers. After he died, we went to his grave on his birthday and we gave him a picture of me on his shoulders so he will always remember me. Now he will never forget me and I will never forget him.

Andru W.

A Special Person

Me and my dog are fast we are super fast. My dog's name is Carter. He is black, and he is little. One day he heard a dog on TV say "ruff." One day he was barking at me. I gave him dog food. It was freezing cold. I remember when I went swimming. I remember we made an alien out of people, out of our hands, head, and feet. I keep swimming til I can float.

Angela H.

My Role Model Jasmine Jones

I remember when my role model left for college.
I remember when her mom tried to hold her cry in.
I remember we were at church.
I remember she left that Wednesday.
I remember that I wasn't ready to leave church, but I had her number.
I remember when I was feeling sad because she is going out of the state.

I remember her school is Kansas State or
Kentucky State.
I remember that she is black.
I remember when she went to college.
I remember when I last saw her before she
left for college.
I remember we were at church.
I remember she loves jewelry.
I remember she loves fashion.
I remember when I was little and I stayed the
night at her house.
I remember she used to babysit me all the
time.
I remember when she stayed the night at my
house and we helped her make some pants.
I remember she put the safety pins in her leg
while my mom was working on the pants.

Angeles S.
French Lick
French Lick is a small town with
a big water park! It has a huge
tube water slide. I like French Lick
because we go there every Christmas
and rent a huge condo, and I
get my own room. Downstairs
there was a huge bathroom
with a hot tub and a sauna
and a shower, and it was
cool. I had a nice view
from my room.

Anonymous

I Remember...

I remember when my mom cut her hair. I remember when I went to King's Island, when I first met my cousin, when it rained hard and stormy. I remember my first day of camp. I remember when I first saw my brother. I jammed my finger. My hand felt like a heartbeat.

I remember first grade. It was easy. My teacher was Ms. Kendrick. I remember my teacher read a horrible book. I went shopping with my grandma. I ate pizza. I got on the roller coaster. I did not feel anything when I got off the ride.

Armundo P.

King's Island

King's Island is the ride of fun
King's Island
Blue, fast
Felt very happy
Little roller coaster
I saw the clouds and the moon
I touched the safety bar
It was raining
I went on the bumper cars
It was along drive to get there and I was surprised when we arrived.
We left at the night time after the loud fireworks

Ayanna P.

Florida

I drove down there in an RV. My cousins and my mom, dad, sisters, brothers, and auntie. We went to the beach. We stayed there for a long time. From the window of my RV I could see the beach. My cousins, sisters, and I ran to play in the water. We built sandcastles out of sand buckets. We collected seashells. We were the only people at the beach from noon to night. My mom, dad, and auntie got in the water with us a little bit later, and we played tag and other games. The waves in the water looked clear blue. It was so pretty. I was kind of scared when it got dark cause I could not really see anything.

Breanna N.

Maw Maw

I remember her jewelry. I remember she is dad's mom. I remember she has dad's voice girl way. I remember her as medium size. I remember her hair is curly, medium size hair. I remember her talk about random things. I remember she was my great grandma. I remember she is a fast person. I remember she is busy on work days. I remember she comes to my house when I get out of school sometimes. I remember we watch T.V. together. I remember she went to my cousin's graduation and got kicked out for screaming. I remember her stylish clothes. I remember her clothes were colorful. I remember her dark eyes. I remember we would go to the store together. I remember she would tell me about how my great aunt got mad for no reason and told my great grandma she was not her daughter anymore. I remember she would tell me stores about my family. I remember I would go see her to make sure she was okay. I remember she likes Quizno's. I remember she lives in a town house and the colors are blue, green white, black, brown, yellow and red. I remember her house is a one bedroom, bathroom, kitchen, living room and decorations with candles. My maw-maw is very nice and colorful. She is my dad's mom. She looks like my dad and talks like my dad.

Brandon M.
Places I Remember
I remember my great grandma saying leave that cotton-picking boy alone.
I remember melting lucky charm marshmallow treats
I remember grilled cheese
I remember daycare
I remember chocolate milk
I remember going to Georgia with my great-grandma
I remember my baseball game
I remember macaroni
I remember baked potatoes
She lives in Georgia
She is nice
She visits a lot
She bought me a dog

She gives me money
I remember going to O'Charleys every Sunday
after church
I remember cutting off the tail of a blue and
green lizard in her bathroom
I remember when she made chicken and rice
yesterday
I remember when she bought a gray bird with
long yellow feathers and biggest and best
whistle ever
I remember my great-grandma's old house
My grandpa's house in Mcdonaugh, Georgia.
My room
In my backyard where there are two sappy
trees that are fun to climb on
My room in our old house that has the little
corner where I played with Buzz Lightyear
toys and action figures when I was four.
The bathroom of my mom's first apartment
where I surprised my mom by walking
without fully knowing how to crawl.
The playground of my mom's old apartment
where I spent a lot of time with my dad.
The tee-ball baseball field at St. Albans where
I first began playing baseball.

I'm From.

I'm from curly dark hair, from grilled cheese
and chocolate milk. I'm from my magnificent
mother Spring Sherise McElroy. I'm from the
potty seat and the high chair that was always
messy after lunch. I'm from Dora the Explorer
and the Rubber Dubbers, from my old dog Alfi
and my bird Cherokee. I'm from the McElroys
and the Russells, from butter baked biscuits

and nasty broccoli. I'm from peas and sweet potatoes, from journeys and stories of adventure. I'm from Chuck E Cheese and Ponderosa, loud music and smooth jazz, from the baseball game where I hit my first homerun, from the hot sauce I put on my chicken. A store there are hot wings are ribs that taste delicious. I'm from 9oz. steak and A-1 sauce the video games and soda. I'm from bully little brothers and annoying my sister. I'm from eat all the skittles and make nasty cookies from waste money, have fun, and rapidly clean when the fun is over. I'm from why you so weird and get out of my room before I throw this remote at you. I'm from shark tooth and Disney World.

Bryce W.

Dad

I remember when my dad help me play basketball.
I remember when we played and fight.
I remember when I went to my dad's house.
I remember when he was very skinny.
I remember when he broke his ankle.
I remember when he came to my first football game.
I remember when he fly me to Florida.

I remember when he took me to Florida. He took me to the beach and to a water park. He took me to the mall and got 4 pairs of shoes. He took me swimming every morning at the hotel. We always did something fun every day.

I remember when he fly me to Florida. He took me to the beach. It was very dirty. And he took me to a water park. He took me to the mall and got 4 pairs of Air Maxes.

Caleb G.

Jimeer

I remember Jimeer. He is my cousin. I have been over to his house. He went to camp in Pike Township. I liked when I played with him. Jimeer played basketball with me. He went to preschool.

I went to Tennessee to see my cousin's house. He has the will.
Me and my friend want to go put-putting one day there. They have a swimming pool there and they have go-kart and they have lots of holes. My mom lets me do ten holes. My friend's mom lets us do all the holes.

Cameron D.

Rayne

1. Rayne wears lots of ponytails in her hair.
2. Se comes to my basketball games everyday
3. Rayne is 3
4. She likes Chicken & Fries
5. She got a Barbie doll for her birthday on June 15.
6. She and her best friend wore tutus
Rayne wore tutus at her tea party, on her birthday, June 15th. I was at the party

The party was good. She had a snowcone machine. The cotton candy machine did not really work.

Camryn A.

Hawaii

I remember seeing all the volcanoes there.
I remember being amazed at beach because it was the first beach I seen with black sand.
I remember running up and down the beach.
I remember each step I took I felt the sand rush between my toes.
I remember laying in the sand and watching the seagulls hover above me.
I remember walking on the coast and feeling the water rush over your ankles.
I remember going snorkeling and seeing all the colorful fish in the water.
I remember hearing ocean wash over the coast of the beach.
I remember it feeling like it was 30° cooler in the water than outside.

Cecilia S.

Teach at Greenbriar Elementary

Miss Kasper is very or pretty small. She is kind but sometimes comes to a too powerful distrustful person. She makes me ferocious and very disconfident in the future. Sometimes it comes to the very delighted action minute and washes away my top feelings.

Miss Kasper is about 5 feet tall with blondish brown hair. At first I liked her because she helps us correct out mistakes and she plans fun activities, like playing store with fake money. She spends her own money for candy and toys for us to buy.

I thought she liked us but she goes in the hallways making us walk eight laps and goes around telling other teachers "Oh, look how bad this class is, they won't stop talking, having side conversations, and stop interfering other classes." This makes me question myself, like "What did I do, and why are you getting all your power over this?"

Rock Bottom

The one Rock Bottom I go to is located on 86ᵗʰ Street. Rock Bottom has dark, dim lights and shading

blinds. There are booths and tables at Rock Bottom.

Rock Bottom kitchen sometimes can get too overheated by

fire. Rock Bottom has a brewery mug club for adults.

Rock Bottom also has television and sports you can watch

During most of the year, Rock Bottom gets kind of cold

because of the heat. When I enter in the building I

feel like I am a very special guest. I hear flammable

fire and feel the comfortable seat that makes me want

to fall asleep or relax. The servers wear suits with a cloth on the bottom and a pad of paper to write
people's orders.

Where I'm From

I am from the dirt and dusty village of home of Port-au-Prince. From the starving to not healthiness of my lifespan. I am from humid and muggy weather to the crush and thumpy village of the capital. I am from the thumbs up to thumbs down of reality. From the sweet hearted birth parents to non-orphan family. From country to the great lakes state.

Chase I.

My Uncle Shawn

My uncle always has a hat that he keeps to himself and wears some of them.
I remember when my uncle took me bowling every 2 weeks.
I remember when my uncle took me to Splash Island.
I remember when my uncle told me not to talk about the trash.
I remember when my uncle tool care of my dog.
I remember when my uncle rode a really big ride at King's Island.
I remember when my uncle helped me with my homework.
I remember when my uncle took me bowling to a really big bowling place and we went on

the disco side.

I remember when my uncle took me to Splash Island and we went.

My uncle always wears a baseball cap has a low hair cut dresses normal and has one girl and has his ears pierced wears glasses sometimes he watches basketball every Sunday he drives a truck to his job. Since the day I was born my uncle has always been there for me. He always likes to do stuff with me. When I was younger every two weeks we would go bowling and over spring break or summer we would always go to King's Island. He has always told me a lot of stuff like how to take out the trash and how to clean up around the house. Ever since I started 1st grade he has helped me with my homework and now I am in 5th grade. Around my 9th birthday I got a dog and me and my mom could not take care of him so my uncle helped us with him. I remember last year we went to King's Island and we rode a really good and big ride. My uncle always wears a baseball hat has a low hair cut dresses normal. And has his ears pierced and wears glasses sometimes he watches basketball every Sunday. My uncle is like my dad to me.

Chris M.

Brother

William.

Tall.

5 foot 8.

But kinda short.

Makes me laugh with funny faces.
Strong.
Has a lot of friends.
Like to play video games with him.
He's cool because he's had all his friends
since kindergarten.

I'm From Macaroni and Cheese
I'm from macaroni and cheese
I'm from the Delta planes to Miami and the
Bahamas to Nasals to Cococay to Key West
I am from candy (Church Philips Temple)
I'm from my mommy, bad toys, and fishing
to pizza from K-mart and video games

I am from Mom, Dad, and Aunt
My mom and Aunt are loving. So is my Dad
Home, Arby's, SFC
I am from Christmas and giving

Davia
My Grandma
I remember when my grandma died. I was
sad. I was crying. And I was five years old
and I never got to see her again. I was very
close to her. I think about her when I look at
her picture. I love my grandma and I always
will and I could not stop thinking about her. I
remember when I went to her funeral and her
reunion and her house and I remember when I
brought her some flowers and I was crying for
a week. I remember when she smiled at me. I
remember when she had curly hair and black

hair and when she dies last year we seen her head stone and I remember when she hold me and I remember when she did my hair. She was fun and pretty and nice. I remember when she had a cute purse. Her name was Marvetta Taylor. She was a nice grandma and she had 6 grandchildren and we all gave her some flowers and she got married and we all love her.

My Dad David

My Dad is so fun and nice and cool and kind and he is a great cook. He is the best dad ever. I love him so much and he plays with me.
He can play soccer with me. He's even my coach. He is tall. He has a beer. He has diabetes. And he is a cool dad.
He is a musician and he can play drums and piano.
His eyes are like mine. We look alike and my Dad's name is David.
He is nice, fun, he takes us skating and swimming and snappers and ice skating and to Chuckie Cheese. And I love my dad so much that he is the best dad ever and I can't let that go. He's nice. He's cool and fun.

David T.
Kaleb

I remember Kaleb is funny.
I remember everyday I will pick Kaleb up to camp because he doesn't have a car.

I remember me and Kaleb go to the movies every Wednesday.
I remember me and Kaleb was in a dance group.
I remember when me and Kaleb met at two years old.
Kaleb's mom and my mom is best friends.
I remember we were at the mall getting some candy from one of those tanks and I remember me and Kaleb played basketball.
I remember when me and Kaleb went to the stories
I remember when me and Kaleb had a dance group there were 4 people David Kaleb Christopher Dayron
we danced to Now Behold the Lamb
We practiced a lot in a church called Phillip's Temple
Me and Dayron Kaleb and Christopher we danced at first Phillip's Temple then another church

Dayron T.

Roller Cave

I remember when I learned how to skate backwards. It was hard, but I learned. I also remember when I learned how to skate. It was very fun. I remember when the music was playin. I go from 8:00 p.m. to 3:00 a.m. It is very fun. People are always on the dance floor. They have a list of people that can jig really good and I am number 1 on the list. Nobody can beat me in the dougie. I am very talented when it comes to skating. My cousin said that he could skate like me but as soon as he orders his skates. He fell on his butt very, very hard. I was laughin so hard I started to cry it was so funny. He had to get starter's skates.

Devan T.

Mom
My mom plays basketball with me at home.
She has black hair.
My mom's name is Coy.
My mom buys me chips.
My mom cooks hot wings.
My mom always wears a dress.
I cook breakfast with my mom.
I like drawing with my mom.
She wears toenail polish.

     At the kitchen table drawing with my mom. She looks pretty in her shorts and shirt.

Grandma
I remember when I showed her my hands and she said those are sports hands.
I remember when she cooked me a hot breakfast.
I remember when she gave me some of her husband's old collectables.
I remember when she bought me some Under Armor football cleats.
I remember when she and her husband took me and my brothers fishing in the hot

summer in Alabama.

I remember when she took me to a water park and the pool had waves.

I remember she took me to a special restaurant when I got to her house.

I remember when I was little she picked me up from school and took me to my football practice.

I remember when she watched me juke everyone on the field and score a touchdown.

I remember she hugged me tight and said I love you.

I remember she texted "Happy Birthday" on my birthday.

I remember she was telling how to be not only like but better than my Auntie and get my Doctor Degree.

I remember she told me I can to anything if I put my mind to it.

I remember she said if you want something you go get it.

I remember I showed her my report card and she gave me a lot of money and said keep it up.

Demetria J.

Chic

I go to a hair salon in Castleton. It is called Chic. There are a lot of other ladies and me. You can also get your nails and feet done at the spa. Brides and bride's maids getting their hair done. Swirly comfortable chair. Has a counter with sink where you tip your head back. I have to sit on hair supply box.

I have a lot of hair supplies. Ms. Kia, she is married and pretty. Talked to other people while she does people's hair. I'm usually asleep. When I wake up she is done and it is done. I'm ready to go.

There's a bakery by Chic and smells like cake and donuts. When we go into Chic, it smells like hair perfumes. The walls are blue. There are two mirrors, one big and one small.

Dance
My skirt was purple. It had big and loud music. Had a guest star to sing. Had lots of support from friends and family. It was for people who had cancer. We had a fashion show. People had people or animal masks. My skirt was like Nigeria skirts out of real fabric. I had lots and lots of fun and it was for a good cause and I love it.

Demetrious J.
Brother
I rode my first bike. Math is fun. My baby brother is crazy. He likes to play Bingo. We got along until he was two. He had a big head. It was the same as mine.

Diarra D.
I am From
I am from fried chicken.
I am from getting bit by my cousin.
I am from Christmas Eve parties.
I am from shortness.
I am from getting corn juice in my eye.
I am from a big red house.
I am from small feet.
I am from Maxine's Chicken and Waffles.
I am from family reunions.
I am from Sweet Baby Ray's barbeque sauce.
I am from Grandma's house where I watch
Betty White's "Off-Their-Rockers" and sit on the
hot porch.

Elijah H.
He was the Best
This poem is about my dad. One time, he woke me up by putting a dog on my stomach and licking me on the face. My dad was in jail 17 times. My dad looks different every day. Right after I said, "Thank you, dad," he said, "No, the dog isn't yours. It's the neighbors', but if they don't take care of it, you can have it." So I'm so impatient now because I really want a dog. But it is actually a puppy. So now I write this story so that I remember.

Elyjah M.

Alex Lopez— He is my Friend

I remember when me and Alex builded a Lego motorcycle and a ship.

I remember when my friend Alex moved I gave him a metal card; it was Pokémon.

I remember when I first met my best friend Alex, Gabi and Mitzy.

I remember when Alex came to my birthday party.

He's very good at shooting games.

He's a good climber.

He plays a good sport.

He's a good swimmer.

He's a good hider.

He has a very funny sister, Gabi.

He has a very nice mom.

He's a good racer.

Our favorite game is Dragon Ball Z.

His favorite food is pepperoni pizza.

Alex moved.

Alex is a good athlete, and his favorite sport is football. We love to play football and other games. We usually play behind the houses. There's a lot of grass there, but we got bored of football so we made a new game called 'super spy ninja robbers.'

I am From a Ceiling

I am from a TV and London. I am from a desk and a wall. I am from a sink and a faucet, soap and hand sanitizer. I am from papers and pencils. I am from cardboard and a Will. I am from

Happy Hollow. I am from Indianapolis. I am from sunscreen, Indiana, Texas, an ice skat-ing rink, Chucky Cheese. I am from a ceiling. I am from legs of a chair. I am from Florida.

Enas H.
Sitting in Silence

My dad takes me to fun places and buys me cool stuff. Usually when he comes back from a far away place, he brings me back a souvenir. Some of the places my dad takes me are Cedar Point or King's Island. There are a bunch of cool roller coasters in the amusement parks, both wooden and metal. One time in King's Island, The racer car we were in lost power just as we were going to come in and they had to power it up. It was very hot in the place we had to sit. We had to sit there for about 10 minutes.

There is a ride in King's Island called The Beast, and it is my favorite. It is very fast going through dark shafts. My hands were gripped on the handles real tight, and my legs were stiff on the ground, and my dad and I were speechless coming off the ride.

I am From Mom, Dad and Tre

I am from Mom and Dad
I am from home
I am from SFC
I am from playing on my parent's phones
I am from Indiana

I am from my house and TV
I am from sweets and candy
I am from my DS

I am from Mom, Dad, and Tre

Mom: loving kind, pampering, smart, cooks Indian
Dad: strong, smart, takes me places, buys me stuff
Tre: annoying, slept over a lot

Sharma week
Sharma week is when my mom's siblings and her family comes to Wisconsin and goes to different places on different days.

Eric P.

I am From
I am from Texas and Indiana.
I am from Florida and from Sonic; he runs fast.
I run fast, too.
In Texas I saw a man throwing
fire with balls in a circle.
It was time for fishing.
I am from catching catfish and eating it.

And I Remember
I remember I had long hair.
I remember I had a Nintendo.
I remember we made a robot.
I remember my dad. My dad's name is Eric. I remember my mom's name.

I remember I had long hair.
I remember my grandma, and I play with my 3-DS. And I play with my Playstation. And I remember Valentine's Day. And I remember my brother is a good climber. And I can swim good.
And my mom is a nurse. And she helped. And I remember my dad had a mustache.
His eyes are brown.
And I can dance good.

Erik B.
McDonalds
I feel happy. I get a lot of toys. I like the food and playground. The slides you have to find your way to the slides and you can also get trapped. I wear my shoes, my shirts and my clothes. My favorite food is chicken nuggets and fries. I go with my grandma and grandpa, I and my mom.

I Swallowed a Marble Once in Preschool
I am from soccer.
I am from pepperoni pizza.
I am from reading magazines about snakes.
I am from playing Wii games.
I am from the television set in my room.
I am from gold and silver.
I am from my grandpa who fought in the army.
I am from my nice mom and my eighteen year-old aunt.

I am from watching Wizards of Waverly Place on Saturday mornings.
I am from Pair of Kings, my favorite show.
I am from Otter Cove Circle.
I am from a house that looks like an L with bricks.
I am from a four-car family.
I swallowed a marble once in preschool.
I go to North Caroline,
where I swim in the lake.
It reminds me of my grandpa in the army.

Hannah M.

I Remember My Room Being Warm and Cozy

My room is my favorite place. I remember my dad painted the room purple and white. I remember the sticker decorations on my wall. I remember not even sleeping in my room as a little girl. I remember my mom always saying, "How does your room get dirty, and you don't even sleep in your room?" I remember my white bed set. I remember watching Disney Channel everyday. I remember making sure I didn't miss Phineas and Ferb. I remember getting a new bed set. I remember getting new furniture. I remember when I would burst in excitement when my mom would tell me we're going to look for a new bed set. I remember sleeping in my room a lot more. I remember my dad redecorating my room. I remember I stopped sleeping in my parents' room at the beginning of 7th grade. I remember my dad making sure my room was spotless before he rearranged it.

I remember sleeping in my bed and not wanting to get up early for school. I remember messing up my room just because I couldn't find anything to wear. I remember looking under my bed and realizing that I have a lot of shoes. I remember going to my room when I wanted to cry. I remember my room being very cool when it was really hot outside. I remember my room being warm and cozy in the winter time. I remember laying in my soft bed when I was really tired. I remember being on the phone with my friend Jada at 2 AM. I remember watching the movie "Lean on Me" and laughing so hard, I almost fell off my bed. I remember over sleeping, so I was late to school. I remember hearing my mom's loud voice as she spoke to my sis. I remember listening to my favorite song.

Sophia Massey-Murff (mommy)

I remember she died her hair a strange color
I remember she took me to Chuck E. Cheese
I remember she put my brother out the house
I remember she bought my sister's Uggs
I remember she bought her car
I remember she cut her hair
I remember she said something funny my grandfather said
I remember she taught that I need to be responsible

I remember she took me to her job.
My mother took me to visit my sister in college
We went to the Kentucky State Homecoming
We went to Penn Station
We helped my sister get dressed for the Travis Porter and Waka Flocka concert
The ride from Indianapolis to Kentucky was long.
I met a lot of my sister's friends
My sister's dorm was noisy.
The girls across the hall were going to different dorms with their friends.
Everybody was making sure their outfits were cute.
Everybody was playing loud music.
My mom and I stayed at my sister's dorm and ate while my sister was at the concert

My mom is a registered nurse.
She always wears scrubs
Her hair is soft and curly.
She doesn't look African American
She has a caramel/reddish skin
She is not tall or short
She has slanted eyes
Her favorite TV show is Law & Order

Herman J.

The Storm was Kind of a Good Thing

I remember my dad taking me to all my sports games.

I remember him being really funny.
I remember him being a very strong person.
I remember him cooking the Thanksgiving
turkey in New Jersey on a very gloomy day.
I remember him wanting to do everything to
help my family.
I remember him buying everything that I
needed to succeed in sports.
I remember him taking me fishing on a bank
out of town.
I remember him helping me catch my first
fish.

I remember him protecting me when I was
young in a thunderstorm at my house at night
when I was very scared. I remember going in
the basement and sleeping there for the whole
night. I remember waking up the next morning and looking at all the carnage. Wondering
if anyone got hurt. There were plenty of fallen
trees and branches. Then we noticed the
power was off and we did not have a
generator for the last 3 days we spent our
time playing words and sitting on the front
porch. I remember thinking that the storm
was king of a good thing that happened
because I got to spend a lot of time with my
family.

Hope L.
My Dog
I remember when my dog chewed my doll's
foot and ate it.
I remember my dog had babies.

I remember my dog is black and white, we called him Oreo.
I remember when she was little and I named her Oreo.
I remember when she was so happy and joyful.
I remember when she played with me and my sisters.
I remember when it was 1,000 puppies.

My dog Oreo had puppies. One of them was named Lucky, and one of them was named Kitty Soft Paws. We have the puppies at home still. There are 1,000 of them! They are always running around the house. Oreo watches her babies.

I am From Being Nice and Smiling all the Time

I am from Chicago,
from my cousins and my mom.
I am from a new house
where the inside looks beautiful.
I am from being nice and
smiling all the time.
I am from pink and red,
from dresses and boots
and ice cream and books.
I am from TV like Sponge Bob Square Pants
and the gardens and flowers
and my best friend and Barbie dolls.
I am from my brother and sister
and the beach and my
house and my Dad

and my skateboard. I am from
my bike and Holiday World and
my food and the pretty
playground and the slide and
the swings and the monkey bars.
I am from basketball and the
football team.

Imari Q.
Marco's Pizza
I love their pizza sticks! I get pop and juice. I
like tea too. My mom and dad take me to go to
Marco's Pizza. I blow on the pizza to cool it
down.

I Am From...
I am from summer soccer,
from chocolate cake and Amiiah.
I am from swimming and playing games with
Tori.
I am from "Shake it Up" and Break it Down"
every day.
I am from swimming with my mommy and a
daddy with no hair and a big belly.

Isaiah D.
My Mom Takes Me to Work
with Her at McDonalds
My mom is seven.

I remember when my mom and I fed the ducks.
I remember when we played football and catch because the coach told us.
My mom makes me chicken nuggets.
We play video games and on my DS.
My mom takes me to work with her at McDonalds.
We make food for the people that come.
My favorite part is that we work and eat.
We stay until it's closed so we can clean up.
I help get the food ready.

I am From the Real Scooby-doo

I am from blue shorts that I like to write on.
I am from ice cream and sour candy and bubblegum.
I am from living with my puppies.
I am from green stickers.
I am from basketball and football.
I am from gospel and jazz music.
I am from ice cream and bubblegum.
I am from basketball with my doggie.
I am from playing with bubblegum.
I am from the real Scooby-doo.

Jaden P.

The Downtown Mall

Dear Carol,

I went to the downtown mall with my mommy and sister to a store called Delia's and bought a blue shirt with a black heart, a white shirt with different print that says "love," a green shirt that says "love is the answer," white capris, a necklace with a heart, and gray duck heart socks.

From Jaden

PS My mom asked my dad and he said no but I asked my dad and he said yes.

Jaelyn W.
My Grandma's House
The reason why I picked my Grandma's house is because her house was the most fun house. I remember her patio with a screen. I remember her turning the oven on to bake the cake and fry the chicken. I remember her room with a lot of glass.

Her patio connected
to her house her
room with tan walls
small house
her house smelled like
chicken. I went over
her house every Sunday
she would watch basketball
with my dad
She wore dresses and
Skirts to church
And if we never came
Over on Sunday she
would get made at us.

I remember crawling under
the table trying to
tickle everyone's feet and
my Grandma would always hit
my hands if I got in trouble
she would tell me to get out of
her house but she was playing
with me and when my cousin
Courtney use to play with me
and we used to fight over
Elmo so they turned on
Sesame Street and then my
Grandma would yell at my dad for changing
the channel.

Jaime J.

Disney World/ Florida

When I went to Disney World it was very very very Hot, it was about 98 degrees. When I was there I saw a lot of characters, but my favorite character is Cinderella, I had a day with her. I went in her castle, and I saw her and prince charming get married.

My Uncle

My uncle works at the hospital.
My uncle had a stroke, but he still
works at the hospital.
My uncle supports me in gymnastics.
My uncle has the same, skin, but he
has a beard and a cane.
My uncle is tall and not married.
My uncle can talk even though he

had a stroke.
He said that the only thing he wanted
to do is be able to run.
Me and my uncle talk a lot.
He gives me money when I have good grades.
He has a frame of a famous boxer and the speech
of Martin Luther King Jr. I have a dream.

Jalen K.
I Remember...
I remember... The first time I was with my grandmother.
We went to Family Dollar.
We bought toy handcuffs.
I was sad when she died.
I went to her funeral.
I remember... When my baby cousin came out of my auntie's stomach.
I remember when my baby cousin came home.
I remember my cousin, she was a girl, was happy she had a baby brother.
My other cousins were 4 and 3.
His name is Jordan and he is 1.
My uncle was happy that he had a new son.
This first time I went to kindergarten I was shy.
My mom is fun because she takes us anywhere we want to go.
I remember when I was with uncle and we went to a race show.

Janai S.

Tennessee

I love it there. It's always warm outside
with good houses. Also, my whole family,
actually half of it were there. We had a
hot tub on the terraces, on two of them.
At nighttime, me and my mom and
grandma would sit on the terrace
at night. "Which side of the country?" you
ask. We were on the Smokey Mountain.

I am Me!

I am from the sweet sound of the Melody's. I
am from a womb of a mother. I am from a
hard-core and loving family. I am from a swim
team and am the smallest ATHLETE. I am from
ham, spaghetti, chicken and broccoli. I am
from the laughter of my friends. I am from fun
screams of excitement. I am from my tree. I
am me!

Jimmesia J.

One Hot Fall Day in September

I remember one hot fall day in September. I
was on the soccer field for gym. I was on
Olivia, Jake and Howard's team. Olivia, Howard, and I were on defense and Jake was the
goalie. Then Howard decided to go back and
help Jake in the goal. They started protecting
the net like their lives depended on it. Olivia
and I were laughing our heads off. When the

game was over we won. Later on during gym Howard told us he was leaving the school. We all got all sad begging him not to leave. After he told us that we stopped talking to him cause he was going us cry. Olivia and I then got over it. Jake, Howard and Jalen were walking into the school and then Olivia and I picked a bunch of pine cones and started throwing them at the guys. After we hit them we ran into the girls' bathroom where they couldn't find us.

With Sparkles

I am from chocolate,
from sweet Snickers and gummy bears.
I am from a big, quiet house.
It smells like laundry detergent
and clean linen.
I am from an irritating flagpole, the
basketball court,
from unacquainted loud boys, and bouncing
balls. I remember
strangers walking on the street with their
dogs.

I am from "Family Matters" in the morning,
from Steve Urkel and Carl Winslow.
I am from hip-hop music
and small headphones,
from days spent at the pool.
I am from Chuck Taylors
with sparkles
and double tongues.

Jordan J.

I remember...

Getting my haircut. Riding my bike. I remember when I drunk juice—first time. I remember when I had an afro. I remember when I had Dad's mustache. I remember I dreamt for the first time. I ate pizza. I was a baby. When I was a baby, I came out red. My hair was wet. I was heavy—8 ounces, 28 inches. It was big, happy tears.

I am From

People: mom, dad, grandma, grandpa
Places: New York, Florida, Baltimore
Food: Ice cream, snow cones, cheesecake, Twinkies, chocolate, oatmeal cookies
Keepsakes: my favorite toys, Beyblades, Dragon Ball Z, video games, PS3 awesome

Jordan Q.

Mom and Dad

My mom has hair, black hair. My dad is bald, but had black hair.
I remember me and my mom went on the Diamond Back at King's Island and the Drop. She was screaming really loud. I remember my dad took me to Xscape.

King's Island

Get on water rides first
You see the Beast

It goes in the woods where the Beast is
I smell funnel cakes
I eat funnel cakes and elephant ears
When I go to King's Island I go on the Drop
with my mom.

Jordan T.

My Friends Came to My Birthday

I remember when me and Nathan went to
Subway.
I remember when me and Nathan played
games outside.
I remember when it was my birthday and all
my friends came to my birthday and we went
bowling.
I remember when I went to Nathan's birthday
and it was a costume party and we played
games outside.
I remember when me and Nathan climbed up
a tree and then we jumped onto another tree,
then another tree, then we climbed down.
I was at his house and jumped on 4 trees.

Bowling Alley

The bowling alley is fun. We get to eat there.
We get to bowl there. We get to eat French fries
and we get to drink Sprite. Oh, and I bowl a
strike and it was my birthday and I got pre-
sents and my friends came.

Joshua P.
Disneyland
I remember when I went to Disneyland. Me and my two sisters and one brother went to the Spiderman ride and got on and had fun.

I was in Texas at my home packing all my stuff to go.

I do not know if we took a plane or a concrete truck.

What I liked best about Disneyland was the ride I went on that went so high I could see all the other rides from the top. I liked how it went straight down to the ground and then in a circle. I was upside down at the top of the circle. My mom, dad, brother, and sisters on it with me. We put our arms out at the bottom and we put them up on the top. I yelled when I got to the top. I said, "Ahh this is so fun. I'm not going to get off. No one can make me." Then I got dizzy, so I closed my eyes and pretended I was sleeping. When I got off everything was moving, but I didn't pass out. And there were characters that I know and that I do not know.

Josiah H.
The Journey
It smells like Mexican
It has half circle door

Circle and square tables
It's buffet
If there is a big group at the top
All I get is chicken
We all go on to the top

The place I love the most is The Journey because the smell of chicken and Mexican food. The walls are caramel colored. They had brown and white circle and square tables like s'mores. When I pull up to The Journey I see the doors have handles that are half circles on both of the doors. When I walk in I smell Mexican foods. When we come to the counter to tell how many people are with us the waiter leads us to our table. Since we always go to Journey with my whole family (10 people) we always go to the top of the small family.

Kaleb M.

David

I remember David we first met in preschool
in little you.
I remember David dance a lot.
I remember me and David are in a dance
group.
I remember David is good at soccer.
I remember David is funny.
I remember David like his chocolate milk.

It Stands For Angel

I am from Mississippi,
From my mama and a visit to St. Louis.

I am from a really, really big house
	where only me, my auntie and my mom
live.
I am from a door on the front and the back,
		from 466b

I am from my TV that's close to my bed,
		where I watch funny shows.
I am from banquet meals,
		the ones that have muffins in them,
		and Taco Bell I like the Dorito ones
I am from the number 39 and 10, I am from
the letter is A, it stands for Angel.

Kennedi A.

Big Waves Were Coming

I remember when I went to Florida. I went to Wet n' Wild. I got in the wave pool and I Wave Pool and went to the deep part. Big waves were coming. It hit me. I thought I was drowning but I wasn't. It was just water splashing in my face.

My Mom

She goes to nursing school.
My mom is 33 years old.
My mom has smooth hair.
She went to New York.
My mom has three kids.
My mom likes to watch.
She likes out of town.

I am From My Planet

I am from my mom that does everything for me. I am from school that I learn things at. I am from high top shoes and favorite skirts. I am from my home that I live in and the bed I sleep in. I am from macaroni and cheese and frosted cookies. I am from my favorite cartoon. I am from King's Island and Holiday World. I am from my bike. I am from basketball and football. I am from God a loving person. I am from my planet.

Lauren H.

My Cousin Alexis

I remember my cousin Alexis. She lives in Texas and I miss her very much.

I remember meeting Janai Shockley. We are good friends. We are great friends.

I remember having great times. I is having so much fun with my friends Janai, Ahlena L, Kily are my friends.

I remember fun times and nice times like that time I've nice times and super fun times a lots of fun times of fun.

I remember having great times with my families.

She is nice and kind. I love her and she is very nice.

I bet she loves me too 'cause we are family. But she is on dad side not mom's. I miss her a lot too. But she is coming for the holiday 4th of July. I cannot wait to see her. I love her. I send her letters and Alexis is my cousin. She is 4. She lives in Texas And she sends me post cards. She shares. We love each other.

I am From Good Times

I am from Indiana. I am from St. Matt, Mrs. Kerin. She has a nice voice. I am from manicures. I am from Juney B. I am from my cousin Reina. I am from painting and finger painting. I am from science. I am from Sky-line and their spaghetti. I am from good times. I am from times with my family. I am from fun.

Lucas Y.

I remember... Places

I remember Municipal Gardens because it was my first time playing. When I was playing there I heard people chanting and people calling plays. The weather was ice cold outside but not inside it was real warm. I was touching the basketball and other people to set picks and to draw a fail. While I was there I was wearing a basketball uniform to be official. There was a whole bunch of people. There were little kids playing tag, other people stretching and waiting for their games, parents being proud for their children. When I was playing I felt nervous but when I get the ball it just goes away because 1) I'm playing with and against my friends, 2) I get to make new friends, and 3) I making not only myself proud but my family also.

I remember Great Times because it's a great place to hangout with friends and family. When I was there I hear kids getting mad for not doing what they want, outside I hear go-karts ready to go, kids having a great time. The weather is sunny and real hot outside and inside is cool with fans blowing. While I was there I felt the steering wheel on the go-karts and I feel the handles on a motorcycle game. I was wearing jean shorts and a pop-eye t-shirt. I was with my mom and 2 of my friend (mostly my 2 friends). I felt great but bummy because we had to leave.

Lyrik E.

Mom

I remember she has brown and black long hair. I remember she is nice. I remember she is tall. I remember when she call me chicken. I remember she is loving. I remember she is sometime in a hurry. I remember she has singles. I remember she has straight hair. I remember she has colorful clothes. I remember she likes to go places with me and my brothers.

I remember the time we went swimming. She splashed me and she taught me how to swim. I was 8. Setting: Broadripple park, big pool, no slides, no diving board.

My Favorite Place

My favorite place is the swimming pool because I feel the warm water and the splashing water. When I walk I feel concrete walls and floors and the hot sun. I hear the birds tweaking splashing water.

When I first get to the swimming pool with my family and friends, I spread my things out and get settled. When I get settled I walk to the pool and jump in it. When I jump in the pool I put my goggles on.

Maiya D.
My Friend Tianna
Sister
Hair in beads
Cotton black shirt
My friend Tianna is like a sister to me
Sometimes she lets me cut in front of her.
She is my friend but she's like a sister to me.
She stays the night. Sometimes we eat popcorn and watch TV. We stay up late. Her mom and my mom are best friends. We wet when we were three but I don't remember it. Here is why I like her so much...
She tells me jokes. She lets me have things. She be's nice to me. When we got older we are going to get an apartment and live together and go to practice.

Mar'Kayla K.
Memories About Dad
I remember when my dad took
me and my brother shopping, and

I picked a very pretty shirt and pants.
I remember my dad took me and
my brother to the roll-arcade, and
we got food. Then I fell, so my dad helped.
I remember when my dad asked me
if I wanted to stay for a night, and
I said yes. We had movie time and had fun.
I remember my dad took me and
my brother to the movies, and we watched
The Avengers and had fun.
I remember my dad got married, and
I was a flower girl, and my brother
was the ring boy. Then we ate afterward.
I remember when my dad was working
and took me with him. He works at
AT&T. He worked at people's homes.
I remember when my dad took me
and my brother and his mom. First, we went
to the store and bought candy. Then, we
went
to the movies and saw Alvin and the
Chipmunks
Squeakquel and ate the candy there.
I remember it was Fathers' Day, and I
called and told him I missed him.
I called to say happy Fathers' Day.

Marquia T.
I am From Having Fun
I am from dancing
I am from skittles
I am from popcorn
I am from Air Max

I am from Levi
I am from TV
I am from laughing
I am from kool aid
I am from being nosey
I am from gum
I am from lime green
I am from Adidas
I am from singing
I am from not sharing
I am from JW Marriot
I am from Elmo
I am from Smores
I am from the circus
I am from Claires
I am from school
I am from money
I am from ice cream
I am from bath and body works
I am more cat daddy
I am from Chris Brown
I am from having fun
I am from 3 bro's and sisters
I am from Dark Brown hair
I am from candy
I am from electronics
I am from Madea
I am from talking
I am from not liking any type of bug; even
butterflies
I am from Reeses
I am from being funny
I am from pineapples
I am from Indianapolis, IN
I am from fruit snacks

I am from cotton candy
I am from riding in cars
I am from Takis
I am from hot fries
I am from Nickelodeon
I am from hot Cheetos
I am from Doritos
I am from wearing mix match socks
I am from Mindless Behavior
I am from Pizza
I am from Hello Kitty
I am lipgloss

Montgomery B.

My Grandma

I remember my grandma being nice to me. She lives in California. I stayed with her for two weeks. I like to play with her. I took my 3-DS. She had fake teeth. We drove to visit her. Her house was purple and pink.

I am From Pancakes, Waffles and Cereal with Milk

I am from a trophy. I am from a medal. I am from a ball. I am from Indiana. I was born in a brick house. I was born in my mom's belly. I am from pancakes, waffles, and cereal with milk. And my favorite cereal is Cinnamon Toast Crunch.

Morgan Wi.

Dwayne (Brother)

My 6 foot, size 17 shoe, 16 year old brother named Dwayne is my hero. He makes me laugh and plays with me. When I am sad he tickles me. He plays basketball and he's going to Vegas for Nationals. I like when he comes to my dance competitions and before I go to dance on stage he tells me good luck just like what I do when he goes to start his games. At school he wears no uniforms. I like to tackle him when he is sleepy but sometimes he get mad but I don't mind. He lets me play on his iPad and I Skype him on mine. I really liked it when he bought a present for me at Christmas and my brother got me a Barbie doll. Now I don't like them but I still have it for when my brother goes to college and comes for visits. I love it when he lets me play with his dog, Mocha, and I really love him.

I am From Dance Studios

I am from a mom named Nicole and a dad name Dewonye. I am from horse stables and HUGE parks. I am from ice cream on Fridays and turkey sandwiches on Wednesday. I am from Franklin Road. I am from Park Tudor School. I am from dance studios. I am from DMPAC (stand for Dance Magic Performing Arts Center) I am from Happy Hollow.

Morgan Wr.

Special Person

My dad Tim bought me a huge TV. It halfway takes up the living room. We watch it together. We watch Law and Order, Austin and Ally, and Lab Rats. We sit very close to each other and he puts his arms around me sometimes. He says why do you watch these funny funny shows? Sometimes after dinner we go to a place named Orange Leaf. My dad is short, funny, good at math, and he works at AA, which means Andrew Academy.

Nakil S.

Space

A.J. neon and me
saw an alien and the alien take A.J.
They eat him. Apples. So good.
And Kayla saw an alien and she
saw aliens too, and they
take her and eat her and she
tastes like apples, too. So good.
And Nakil wuz there. The aliens' friend.

Nehemiah A.

My Friend's House

Playing on his PS3
Playing with Nerf guns
Playing with his swords
Walking their dog
Playing with his friends

When I spend the night at my friend Matthew's house we hide and find each other when we play Nerf. I bring my Nerf guns to his house so we have more choices. I pick small ones and ones that shoot far. We hide in his room and downstairs. Sometimes I catch him by surprise and shoot him. I yell, "Got you." He says, "No, you didn't," because he didn't feel it. When we finish we watch TV in the living room. They have really cool things: a big flat screen TV. He has Netflix and his Wii. In the other room he has his PS3.

Nia D.

People

I remember my friends Terryn and Amya. I like to play with them outside and inside. I see them at camp. Amya has beads in her hair, Terryn has braids. We play hungry hippos! And we get on the swings! We made a pulley at Mrs. Carla's.

I see them at camp. We went to the movies and we eat lunch. We write together and we read together. We swim at camp. We do art with a heart.

Noah H.

Special Places

When I was at Dave and Buster's we first ate something. I would order grilled cheese, pizza, a cheeseburger then I would first go play and try to get some tickets. I would go and get stuff and when I was done I saw how much tickets I'd have. I go to see what I could get. My favorite thing there is the ticket thing. It is a spinner where your goal is to get 1,000. It has different colors and red is 1,000. There's a picture of a pirate. Sometimes the line is long and sometimes it is short.

Rafael S.
Conner Prairie History Museum
Me and my dad drove to Conner Prairie and when we were there we got a membership. One half is inside and the other half is outside. So we went to the Civil War part. There was a mini theater. We waited for someone to come. While we waited, some person showed us and some other people a real bayonet and musket. He showed us how a soldier would put the bayonet on the musket. Then someone came and opened the doors for us to go see the movie. After that they started shooting a Civil War musket, but I did not want to, so me and dad went to the Native American part. I entered a throw the tomahawk contest and if you got all 5 tomahawks to hit the wood target you won. I tried and only got 4 of them to hit the target but it was still fun. So then we both went into a trading store. There were real animal skins and an old-fashioned lantern and a raccoon hat and a musket with a cut barrel. A person told me that Natives cut the barrels and I thought that

was odd. Then we went to a blacksmith shop. There were horseshoes and swords. It was so cool. I heard a loud popping sound and I jumped. Then I saw it was a musket.

Roderick W.
Special Person
I remember Jimeer Jackson. Jimeer has an X-box 360 in the basement. He is funny and silly. He liked to play sports. He is 9 years old; he is going into third grade. He went to summer camp.

Roman D.
Mexico
When I went to Mexico with my cousin Tyree, my mommy, and my daddy, it took us 2 airplanes. Then, on one day while we were still in Mexico, we went to a place called Aqua World. Then, I took a picture with a parrot. Then we got in an area where there was a large crocodile but we didn't see it. Then we all went under a bridge. Then I saw three pirate ships. The three pirate ships had a cross bone flag and were really cool then we went to the island. The island was called Isla Mujeres. After we all hung out on the island for a while, I snorkeled 30 feet and saw a lot of fish including a starfish. When we got done snorkeling, I took a picture with a shark, drove in a golf cart, and went to a place where

2 iguanas were fighting. I got a hammerhead shark tooth on the island.

Roy B.
I Remember...
I remember when I would go to my granny's house, I would go to the backyard to try going up top of the hill to go over the wall.
I remember when I went to Disneyland.
I remember when I went to uncle's house.
I remember when I went to Game Stop.
I remember when I first went to school.
I remember when I went to the beach.
I remember my first visit to my first school, it looked pretty old when I first saw it but the inside was pretty good when I checked. By time I made friends with the other kids and met a friend who was more than just a friend to me, her name was Clara. But I was still a little kid back then; now I'm in a new school with new friends, but I'll still remember my old friends, especially Clara.
Clara and I were best friends, we were the only people that would ever talk to each other. We didn't know each other much but we were both ok with it.

Shania B.
Uncle Dee
My uncle Dee lives in California. He comes to visit not that much. He chases me and his girlfriend around.   His girlfriend's name is

Quanisha. He's tall and thin. We have a lot in common. We both make friends easy. He tickles me and I scare him by hiding and jumping out at him. He takes me to the movies. I never want him to leave.

Shawn F.

Bridgeport Elementary

My 3rd grade teacher, Mrs. Young, draw on your desk. Miss Chlodo has a chalkboard and a white board. Where I sit is by my teacher's desk. My desk is touching her desk. Who I sit by is my best friend Caleb Kelly (it is kind of chilly). The walls are white and shiny. She has an alphabet and numbers and pictures of her kids and one time they came in! She has a lot of games and a reading corner. She has two red chairs that are comfy and smooth. There are computers on the computer desk. My teacher takes us to the restroom in 10 or 5 minutes. She is actually kind of mean and kind of nice.

Shekinah F.

I am From...

I am from toys in the kitchen.
I am from lots of bubbles that I pop in the sink.
I am from Sketchers Twinkly Toes.
I am from Gameboy DS and Mario Kart.
I am from my "U" book and umbrellas.
I am from a white house with an upstairs and downstairs.

I am from Shanna and Sanox and Shamn and Shialoh.
I am from tumbling.
I am from macaroni, cheese, and grapes.

Simone M.

Spa La La

I remember mom cheering me up when I didn't want to try out for the solo in dance.
I remember mom taking blame for me when I was in trouble.
I remember mom making a sandwich for me in the kitchen while on the phone.
I remember mom standing by my side when I had to sing in Atlanta.
I remember when mom took me to a spa to celebrate Honor Roll.
Never wants to give up.
Very busy at work.
I remember when mom took me to the hospital because she didn't know what was going on with my hands.
I remember going to the mall with mom to have a girls' night alone.
I remember mom being the team mom for my cheerleading team.
Mom has always been special to me. She has always been there for me when I let my head hang low, and will still be there. My expectations are always high when she's there to support me when either I have a softball game, cheerleading practice or a game, and dance practice. Mom's about 5.8 feet tall. She has curly hair and wears glasses.

Stephanie M.
Chicago
I remember going to Chicago with my mom. Last year my mom and I went to Chicago together. It was a fun drive there because I got to learn more things about her when we got to Chicago.   First, we checked into our hotel. Then we took our bags up to our room.

We were either going to go to the children's museum or the zoo. We decided to go to the children's museum because it was too could outside for the zoo. After we left the children's museum, we went outside and got on the Ferris wheel, and we got back to the hotel and decided to walk to the Cheesecake Factory.

Once we were done eating, we walked back to the hotel. We talked and then we went to bed. The next morning we went shopping. Then we drove back to Indy. We had planned on staying in another hotel, so when we got there we bought a pizza. Once we were done, we went downstairs and swam. Once we were done swimming, we went back upstairs, and my dad my dad was there, and an hour or two later we went to bed.

Sterling M.
My Grandmother's House
It smells like fresh baked Double Chunk Chocolate Chip Cookies when you just walk in. She gives me six to start with so I get a warm glass of milk and watch TV. So I thought she

could TV with me so she said yes. So she always had this great smile—pure white teeth. And I always pet Cocoa (her dog). She's so hyper and lovable, and Cocoa's "male mate" Brownie also lovable too, so they always have to be together and never apart. I love spending the night over because cousin Chance spends the night with me, Cocoa, and Brownie. First we wrestle, then we both play secret spies for a midnight snack and my grandfather is not the best overnight guard. So we just walked right past him and we got fruit snacks, soda, a lot more double chunk chocolate chip cookies (now with chocolate filling). We both grabbed as many as we could (26 each). In the morning grandpa was confused because there were 52 cookies and now they're gone.

She has a good personality. She never said no to positive or needy people. I loved the way she cared for people and their needs and then hers. She would always be a good role model. She will let you do anything. Just tell her where you're going, how long you're staying, and where it's at. The thing that changed me was she died in March 2010. She will always be a heartwarming person and she will always be a good person.

Sydney B.
When I Fell off the Stairs
I remember when I always use to have the same dreams at night and they were in color like in real life. The place was over at my grandmothers. In the dream I fell down the

stairs and it made me scared. And at the end of it I was in pain and I cried.

I remember when I learned how to ride a bike without training wheels. I remember when my mom made the best chicken pot pie. I remember when I got kinki braids by the Africans. I remember when I always had dreams about me falling down the stars. I remember when I went to Louisville for my family reunion, and I drove there. I remember when I visit my family that I never seen before. I remember when I bought rings from the mall.

Taiche R.

When I Went to Chicago

I remember when we went to Chicago for my birthday and it was Me, My mom and brother. It was very cold. We went there in April and at night it was very beautyful and then we got on a boat and they were telling us every thing about Chicago. I was wearin' a red coat with South Pole on the back. There was this one lady who was taking Pictures close to the edge of the boat and when she sat down she dropped her phone in the water because it was sliding in the under the chairs but as we were going there was a big bright ferris wheel. It was very colorful. Lights so many and when the boat had to turn this brild landed and I woo like very big so this little girl went down stairs screaming and her mom just sat there so her brother can get her so when it was time to go there was this hotel and the room was wow. There was a lot space full of nothing and we had a good view of the apple store that was there so then when I went in the bath room. The light was very bright like blinding, so I just went with my brother to get some ice. As we were on the boat there was people waving at us above and this lady just yelled.

Tamara V.

I am From...

I am from Washington Square Flocker
I am from my home room 207
I am from church on Forest Manor
I am from chicken nuggets at MacDonald's
I am my grandparents
I am from the basketball court
I am from the Rush-Moore reunion
I am from big Indianapolis home
I am from kriss-kross applesauce
I am from a big red house in Indianapolis
I am from the point guard on bb team
I am from GGMBC—Greater Gethsemane
Missionary Baptist Church
I am from loving grandparents
I am the SFC camp
I am MLK Street Church
I am from the assistant pastor's
granddaughter
I am from blue berry bushes.

Taylor B.
My Family

I am from a house that is yellow and made of bricks. A house that is very loud. A lot of laughing and a lot of screaming (which is mostly me and the little girl)

I am from a little girl (loud and small) but is a true diva has been a diva her whole life. Has an attitude like she is the queen of the world, her own fashion from matching hot pink to lime green and from matching skirts to jeans. She loud and thinks she many things from a singer, to dancer, to soccer player. She very loud like she speaking to a crowd from a cute funny laugh to crying that sounds like she dying.

I am from a man (short and cool) been in my life since the age of two been funny his whole life. You may say he is crazy but I love him dearly (even though he not my dad) He makes me laugh from his singing, to dancing, from even making jokes. The man who has three tattoos, one on each arm and one on his chest. He ride a grayish black Malibu that can start by itself. He is from a student, to a brother, to a son and to a husband but to me he just a short crazy man.

I am from a mom (tall and funny), has a loud laugh and is always making jokes. She went from a college student to a mother of two, and a wife with a small and funny man. A woman who is the peace maker that is very sweet and has the weirdest dances I've ever seen (but a funny way). It's like Carlton on

Fresh Prince of Bel-Air with crazy facials but that is the lady I love.

I am from a family that crazy but I love them dearly.

Terryn P.

I Remember...

I remember Elkhart.
I remember Indiana Beach.
I remember Merrillville.
I remember Wetzel's Pretzels.
I remember my room.
I remember going to my grandma's house.
I remember Fazoli's.
I remember Applebee's.
I remember Incredi-plex.
When I go to Elkhart when it's hot we go to the beach. It has a big water slide and a sand playground and an ocean. Me and my cousin Mackenzie play. WE found clams and in the inside it looks like mayonnaise. I have lots of cousins. About 1293060040000000000 of them. And Elkhart has a moat.

Tianna C.

Michigan

When I went to Michigan, I met my four cousins. We went to the beach. The beach had warm sand from the sun and it felt soft and kind of cold at the bottom. Me, my mom, and my cousins (Lola, Tom, Jemmy, and Kelly) all made a big sand castle and made a hole for the lake and the wind blew most of it away. We were mad but we went to play in the pool. When I left I was sad. It took us 2 whole days to get there and back! When we were at the beach I saw colorful rocks and I took my pail and collected many rocks.

Tre C.
Florida
Enas is walking out, side-moving, fast. Is walking there with me and swimming at the beach and surfing and my mom and dad were still at a hotel. Wille, me, and Enas were at Florida having fun. It was fun at Florida. We went to the movies and we were so excited. The buildings are very tall. It looks like it's touching the stars.

Trinity S.
I am From...
I am from the mall.
I am from John Strange School.
I am from Allisonville Road.
I am from mindless behavior.
I am from basketball.
I am from my brother who cares for me.
I am from the St. Florian Center.
I am from my mom that I love.
I am from a dance team.
I am from Aeropostale.
I am from purple, blue, black, white, red.

I am from a candy lover.
I am from my Aunt Shawn who gave me my
American Girl doll.
I am from a chocolate store and a nice hotel
in Chicago.

Trinity P.

Ricky Rocky

I remember...
playing with him giving him dog treats.
He has soft gray fur.
We got Rocky when he was two.
He's like a sweet cuddly toy.
He can ride on a skateboard.
His collar is golden, it's made out of gold.
He likes to run and jump.
When the doorbell rings and someone tries to
come in, he jumps and barks, and he's scared
of new people.
I remember he jumps really high in the sky.
He runs too fast that I can't catch him.
We jump together and run together.
He loves to lick me and I give him food.
He jumped and when he jumps I catch him.
He makes me Happy.
On August is his BirthDay.
I love him.
He is the Best Dog. I Love him so much. I will
do anything for him because I will never
forget him.

Vonesha D.
Lemonade Sale!
I was outside my house.
I was really hot, like 90 degrees F.
My cousin was helping me.
My neighbors were selling things they did not want.
I gave half of my money to Riley Hospital.
I made $350.00.
I was selling raspberry lemonade, regular lemonade, orange lemonade, strawberry lemonade, grape lemonade.
I had to give some of my money to my cousin because she helped me.
I had a large sign that said "Vonesha's Amazing Lemonade."
I had a tip for Riley Hospital.

Wesley C.
Tennessee
In Tennessee, I went to my uncle Greg's, and I swam in the pool.
I ate dinner, and I played my DS on the way home.
We took our car.
There was a trail in the woods.
His house had stairs.
He had a big TV; he had everything, and his house was blue.

Wesley G.

A Special Person

I had my cousin spend the night over my house and we played the game and ate ice cream and we went outside to play some football. When I finished my team won the football game. One of the team people on the other team...

William M.

Majesty of the Sea

After lunch my friend called and said he was going tonight. It was 12:00 and my mom woke me up and told me that Jaden called, so I put on my swimming trunks and met him at the pool. His dad is a photographer so we dove into the pool and he took a picture of us and then my dad jumped in with us and started swimming with us. Then we got out, went to our room, and put on our pajamas and went to sleep. I woke up and sailed to Key West. We took pictures of many things we saw that were interesting. We rode a trolley tour of Key West, got back in the ship, and got ready for dinner. Our waiter was really nice. He would make everything perfect and just the way we wanted it. The last day we went to Starlight Diner for breakfast. Then we exited the ship and took a taxi to the airport, took a plane to Philadelphia, and one to Indiana, and we drove home to go to bed.

Zion J.

Fishing

Wow this lake is so big I say as I glare at the huge greenish blue lake. The weather was just right it was is sunny day with a light breeze perfect fishing weather. I couldn't wait to get all of the fishing gear out because I had a feeling that today was gonna be a good day. Me and my family have been planning this trip for a whole week to go up to north Indiana to go fishing. Everyone was wearing old clothes old shoes and caps to keep the sun off of us. As my dad is getting fishing poles ready I go explore. I walk around the lake and find many different species of plants and animals. Then my dad calls me and we are reading to start fishing.

I yelled finally because I was so eager to start. I grabbed my fishing pole, put a worm on it, and casted right into the middle of the lake. I remember doing this countless times in a row with no fish I started to get a little frustrated and then I caught a decent size catfish. I remember listening to the catfish splashing, trying to fight its way away from me then I reeled it in. That's when it all started.

For more than 120 years, Concord Neighborhood Center has been a corner-stone of the south side Indianapolis community. Through social services and educational, recreational and cultural enrichment opportunities, it touches the lives of approximately 4,000 people each year. The Summer Day Camp offers students, ages 5-13, an array of activities that involve education, health & fitness, art, music, and the enhancement of social skills. Its overall goal is to provide an engaging environment that accelerates achievement during the months when learning losses most frequently occur.

Middle school students in this year's Writers' Center poetry project explored their world while learning about what makes a good poem: specific details that appeal to the senses, imaginative compar-isons, and language that takes delight in how it's expressed through sound and rhythm. At each session, students contributed lines to a collaborative free verse poem and then wrote their own individual piece. Volunteer Patricia Cupp and interns Michael Baumann, Jessica Tatum, and Vienna Wagner served as important mentors during the writing process, giving encouragement and asking questions that directed students toward specificity and careful word choice.

Shari Wagner

Concord Neighborhood Center

The Playground
It's where I sat on the bright orange swirly
slide
      and went across the jungle gym
      like a spider monkey,
where my friends and I hung like possums
      by our feet on the monkey bars,
where there was a swing and the air
      blew my face,
where I heard old and young kids screaming
      in happiness or pain,
where I listened to ropes slapping the ground
      and learned to Double Dutch, to chant:
      Ice cream, Ice cream, cherry on top,
      How many boyfriends have you got?
It's where I slid down the green pole,
      my hands blistered with dirt.

"Self-Portrait with Straw Hat" Vincent van Gogh, 1887
He has a ginger beard
and a yellow farm hat
the color of hay and the sun.
He's looking in the mirror
and seeing his ear,
thinking he should not
have cut it off.
His lips and ear are red as blood.
His neck is wrinkled
like when a leaf
falls on the river
and the ripples spread out.

"Starry Night"
Vincent van Gogh, 1889
The rotted out tree
looks like dark fire
coming over the town.
The tree looks like the shadow
of the city.
The stars are like wind
or waves of baby suns.
The sky looks like oil pastels
forming together.
The sky is a machine
pulling taffy.

All of this is going on
but you hear no sound.

Alondra A.
Strolling on the Streets
Strolling through the busy streets,
smelling the greasy pizzas
and yummy glazed donuts,
walking as if I was a turtle who
doesn't know where to go,
beside me, my little brother
speaking as I act like I care.
Blue skies and blueberry pies! Yum!
BEEP-BEEP! as the horn of the car went.
Not so soothing or chaotic time,
but it was just fine

Azhure S.

Tree Stand

Nice is the best way to put it.
Calm and beautiful is the
best way to picture it.
The woods are wonderful.
The sounds of the animals, of the
birds are like songs,
and the sound of the
running
and the sound of
the snake slithering
in the green. Rushing
water is the most
beautiful sound
to hear.

Hannah

Working hard, being crazy
When you see her you become
happy

Playing, running, don't know
What she is doing.

When she is around all you hear is,
"Really?"

Kobe

When he came I knew we were best friends.
I knew he was going to be just like me when I
was a baby.

When they got home and I first looked at him,
it was like looking in a mirror and seeing
myself as a baby.
Just screaming my lungs out.
I pick myself up and then I look away and
look back.
Then I see the most beautiful eyes looking
into mine.
Then the cry is starting to fade away. It was
quiet for a long time.
Right there and then I knew he was a keeper.

And now he is two and me and him are best
friends.

Breanna S.
Biggest Present
Walking slowly into a room,
can't see cause my eyes were closed.
I hear noises; a family plays tag.
I am getting close and closer.
Then my eyes open;
I see the biggest thing I have ever seen.
It was wrapped with pink Dora paper.
As I was poking it, trying to open it, thinking
of what it was,
ripping it off so fast, paper was on the floor
Then you saw it....
It was big and bright pink; it was a My Little
Pony set.

Chai B.

My Big Bro

Whenever I pull
up in front of his house, or he
pulls up in front of my house, I
get this feeling. A feeling that
I don't normally get when
guests come over to my house or
when I go to their house. When
I get to his house or he
gets to my house, I can't believe
my eyes. I think I'm dreaming
and I wipe my eyes multiple
times. I've even tried pinching
myself.

When I have to leave, or
he has to leave, it's like the
world is beginning to turn dark.
Most times I won't see him
for another year.

Lost in the Store Again

Mom! As I'm wandering through
the store, I listen for my brother's cries.
Chai! Chai! Where are you?
I haven't heard a word out of my
mom. As I'm wandering, I say to myself,
"Darn it; I shouldn't have wandered off."
I call to my brother one last time,
"Ezra!" He yells back, "Huh" as my
mom zaps to Ezra, "Shut up, boy."
Finally, I get close and find they
are nowhere to be found. My heart

drops to my feet, my breathing
speeds up, and, as I look around,
nothing is to be seen except racks
of clothes and the plain, dead, white
square tiles I walk on, and strange
people look at me as if I'm crazy.
As I look over my shoulder,
I see this tall, pale figure with
blonde, curly hair, wearing a blood
red sweater. My walk speeds up,
but not fast enough. The figure
reaches out and rests its hand on
my shoulder. I freeze and a soft
voice as if birds were singing said
to me, "Do you need help finding
your mother?" I nodded. "Come
with me to the front office, and
we'll call her."

Diamond S.

Paris

I come to a big city
with all the traffic
and many people walking.
My friends and I are finding our way
to the Eiffel Tower.
We see white roses,
pigeons cooing on the street
and dogs barking.
I walk by a bakery with bread
that smells like coffee.
We finally get to the red, white, and blue
lights
on the Eiffel Tower.

We take pictures and climb the tower.
We see the whole city full of lights.
I wish this would happen again.

Dylan C.

Austin

My brother playing Xbox
noisy and obnoxious on MW3
always talking trash.
He wears Elite sox and Aeropostale shirt
brown hair fresh cut.
Later he fishes.
He hates tuna like people hate dog's breath,
only one in the family that can't cook.
He's always happy with his Xbox,
talking to anyone in the world

Jadan G.

What My Old Room Reminded Me Of

I remember the looks of my
old room. Purple and blue were the
colors of the walls. The way the
covers felt reminded me of being held in
my grannie's arms before she died.

Flipping off my bunk bed reminded
me of the first time I ever
jumped into the pool. Every time I
looked out my window I could see
me a new future every time.

Throwing the ball at that
lamp reminded me of the first time
my parents showed me my new
room. I was the prettiest and smallest
thing in there.

After a while my parents
brought my first little sister home.
She came crying into my little brown
arms. She was littler than me. I
put her to sleep on the couch. As I
was looking at her I also fell
asleep.

Sienna

Sienna is the shortest, fattest,
prettiest little girl I know. She reminds
me of a panda.

Her favorite color is light leaf green
and she always wears something
that has green on it.

She always tells her own
jokes. She makes sounds like
sm sm sm sm sm sm boom.

As beautiful as she is, she
is very crazy. The way she
runs cracks me up. While she is
running, she looks like an elephant.

Jasmine A.

Preschool

I was sitting down
in my small blue
chair at my table.
Then, suddenly, "knock, knock,"
my mom came in, taking
baby steps. I also noticed she
had my baby brother. My brother
was in his beige
little baby basket. From far
away, my brother looked like
a small, fat pimple.

My friends were yelling and
singing, "Who wears short shorts?
I wear short shorts."

After ten minutes passed
by, it smelled like poop.
I had found out my friend
got scared and pooped in her
purple pants.

I went over and rubbed
my hands against the
baby basket. It felt smooth
like plastic.

The hands on the clock
were moving one by one,
ticking like wind, swooshing
second by second.

My friend was rushing

down the hall as if she
was the wind. Friends
were chasing after one
another like hungry ants fighting
over food.

Mrs. Paula
Wearing her pink Concord
Neighborhood Center t-shirt,

with her brown hair
and shorts like bark,

Mrs. Paula dresses
casual like me.

The color blue is
cool like her.

She helps kids with
their problems at
Concord like a therapist.

I've helped her with
work, and I am
also in her older
group called
"Now for the Future."

When she enters
the room, I feel safe.

Separation

Crying as I watch
  them fight, yelling and
    screaming like
      wolves at night.

She left the house and
  never came. He said
    it was her little
      game.

She came the
  next day, but I
    just sat there in every
      way.

As I cried, my dad cried, too.
  We all were
    sobbing, saying
      boo-hoo.

That day I will
  always remember
    like my mom's and dad's
      phone numbers.

Jennifer M.

Mexico's Beach

I remember hearing the
birds over the ocean flapping their
wings and the soft sand
between my feet.
I remember hearing

the sound of children
running and making the sand be carried
with the wind and smelling the
fresh air that rushes
through my face.
I remember the joy
of the child who
won the sand castle contest
and the beautiful sound of
the seashells that appear
in each wave.
I remember the families
going in and out the
beautiful blue sea.

John S.

Great-Grandmother's House

When I walk into the kitchen I see a hexagon
table and chairs.
On the wall is a singing pendulum clock.
I wash the soft blue berries and the purple
grapes and put them on the tray.
I stir the chicken, peas, and noodle soup in
the pan on the stove.
I mix cherry Kool-Aid and pour it into mugs.
Then great-grandmother and I have a
delicious lunch.

Florida Jordan

Florida is dead.

Florida had light brown hair
like pancakes.

Florida was old and died at
age eighty-three.

Florida treated everyone with
respect.

Florida and I used to watch
The Price is Right and
Animal Planet.

Florida and I cooked
together, and she taught me.

It feels nice when I
can sit down and talk to
her.

Florida loved sweet potatoes,
especially when my mom
made them.

I would like to say that
Florida will rest in heaven and will
not have to suffer breathing
with tubes and machines.

Camp Town
Six of us connected in orange and red canoes
paddle as a team to catch up with other
groups.
We're getting splashed with water guns
and cold creek water. It's hot outside and
we're sweating.

We crash into a tree branch and try to get
free.
I'm wet from head to toe.
We splash our own teammate Mrs. Paula in
the face.
She screams, "I'm going to get you, John."

Laurin W.

The Mall

I like going to the mall.
I love walking through
the food court
and smelling tacos,
cinnamon pretzels, and different
kinds of meat from different
places. I also hear the popping
sounds of the skillets or
the beeping of the microwaves.
When my mom pulls me away
from the food, we make our
way through the food into the
stores, passing people spraying
perfume on people that smells like
roses and peaches; it's a glorious
smell. When we walk into the
stores, the clothes look like a
rainbow threw up on them. The
sounds you hear are of the cashier
checking out your purchases, or, across
the walkway, you hear children
laughing. Then it was six o'clock, time to
go. As my parents and I drove away, I fell
asleep.

My Cousin
When we were little we used
to dance. We had a particular
dance. It was ballroom dancing. We
would always go over to my grandmother's
house and dance on her old squeaky
floors and push the buttons on
the piano while our grandmother made
us popcorn with extra butter. The
house smelled like a movie theater
and so we put in a movie. It would
be her choice, of course. She always
picked Barbie, and after that we always talked
about what we want to be when
we grow up. She wanted to be
a star. I never said anything.
I always listened to her.
Di died of cancer at six.
Those were the good memories.
It was a sweet precious time that
no one or nothing could take
away.

Hide and Seek
When I arrived at my grandmother's house,
my cousins were hiding.
While I opened the squeaky gate decorated
with silver dogs, everyone jumped out.
Then as I galloped on the cracked sidewalk
while I said,
 "Step on a crack, break your mother's back,"
I raced into my grandmother's house and
jumped through her door.
The whole house shook and I didn't care.

Then I threw my things on her old tattered
couch.
I took off my shoes and ran outside.
I slid on the rough grass and laughed.
We played the whole day.
And as the silent sunset became no more,
I ran inside and played some more.

Michelle P.

A Summer Day

As we walk outside, the sun is
like a dragon breathing fire on us.
We play basketball forever and ever,
forgetting all about the heat.
I quench my thirst with water from the hose.
When the ice cream truck comes
we beg our parents
for money to get ice cream
that melts.
As we have water balloon fights,
girls against boys,
others see and come to join.
Then the sun goes down.
We feel the wonderful breeze
sweeping in.

Noah C.

Red

I remember the fire's crackle
and connect it to what red is.
I remember when my grandma
would cook the meat on

the grill, and the taste
was like how I imagined
red tasted. I remember at
my old house that
there were a lot
of cardinals screeching like
a banshee because of
our cats. I remember getting
red rubber balls and playing
dodge ball, the dodge balls hurling
like a speeding rocket.
Whenever I look at
home, I know that
the sight, taste, sound, and
texture of red
would be there to
comfort me.

During La Plaza's Leadership Institute for Latino Youth (LILY) summer program, the Building a Rainbow memoir writing is used to bolster social inquiry, creative questioning, and self-confidence. Students are asked to explore meaning within their communities, how their actions impact those around them, and to articulate thoughts and desires. Above all, we play with words and explore the power of expressing ideas and documenting events.

Each LILY writing group is asked to develop a group identity, a name to share with the world. After careful deliberation and a round of vigorous voting, this year's group selected Monkeys with Typewriters as their collective moniker. In addition to the selections within this anthology, more compositions are published in the Monkeys with Typewriters' blog at monkeystypewriters.tumblr.com

Many special thank-yous go out to the interns who sit, write, and share alongside the students: Amy Demien, Corrie Herron, Brett Hiatt, James Figy, Zhenzhen Liu, and Caroline Wilson (you've taught more with your actions and questions than you'll likely ever know). Thank you to the staff at La Plaza and the Writers' Center of Indiana for working together in realizing a vision of empowered and brilliant young minds.

Mark Latta

Aylin J.
I Remember...
I remember when I was in the 4th grade, I went on a trip. It was with my elementary school. There were three classes of 4th graders. Each had its own bus. The trip was to Louisville Baseball Museum and Marengo Cave. I had to wake up at 5:00 am. We had to meet in the elementary school at 6:30am! The buses weren't like school yellow buses, they have fur and a TV inside. The Louisville baseball museum was in Kentucky. The trip went fast. We could sit with our friends. Nintendo DS's were famous back when I was in 4th grade (which was almost 4 years ago) all we did was play and talk. In the museum they had a workshop of how to make baseball bats. They had a hall of fame, history of baseball, famous people from baseball history. I took pictures. Then we went to Marengo Cave.

The cave was dark, cold, and quiet. It was so cold that you had to wear a jacket. There were stalactites sticking out. I wanted to touch one but it was against the rules. Along with the coldness, there was a bit of water. Once in a while there was a tour guide pointing things out. There was a wall full of pennies. They each gave us a penny. I threw it up but I lost sight of it. I thought it was stuck to the wall but I seriously doubt it. The tour guide told us the history of the cave. It goes: in the 1880's (I think) this boy and girl were playing and they found a mysterious tunnel. They went back home to get a candle and explore the cave. They went back home to tell their mother.

They owned the property. They wouldn't ever turn down the people who wanted to buy it. The family owned the cave. In the 1900's (I don't remember when) the family sold the land to explorers who wanted the land. The family never went inside the cave though so eventually the explorers explored the cave. In years, they finally decided to open it to the public...

We left the cave. We got to the elementary school around 7 or 8pm. I was exhausted as a savior. I bought a cute little teddy bear. I also got in a tunnel. It was dark and hot. You had to find the exit. Many kids couldn't because it was hard. I went in front of my friend and found the exit.

Aylin M.

Mexico

Mexico in Juarez, rumors took over my mind. Gang violence, robbers, drug dealers, frauds. My emotions seemed to be playing a game of tag, rushing all at once and then disappearing. But once reality hit, it was a whole different story. Beauty took over Juarez. An enormous newly constructed mall, well dressed crowds of people. Then—BAM!—Army tanks! Soldiers! Suddenly the game began in my head once again. All guarding entrances to their nearly beloved government building waiting for someone to make a move. No one ever did. Homeless people in the street begging for pesos. Its kinda depressing to think about. Makes you think about how lucky you actually are.

Cheesecake

The scrumptious taste, the endearing smell, the burst of flavors in your mouth when you've taken the first bite, like someone set off fireworks in your mouth. The creamy texture, the perfect sequence... pie crust, cheese cake, strawberries, bread crumbs, cheese cake. Or as I would call it, a piece of heaven.

Dulce L.

I Remember...

I remember this weekend that on Friday my lights went out. My brother was entertaining me, since we couldn't watch TV. An hour passed and still no light, so we fell asleep and when we woke up the lights cam back so we ordered pizza. We also watched a movie and then went to sleep.

On Saturday I went to work for 3 hrs and then left to buy my guest book. I hanged out with my friend Iris and then went back to work. At work I started working on my center pieces and went home after that.

On Sunday I was at home cleaning and painting my room. I painted my walls white but we are going to repaint it to light pink. I got new curtains and a new lamp. My curtains are purple and my lamp is pink. I went to mass afterwards and talked to the priest about my party.

Later on my brother and I went to his friend's house and we played Wii and took pictures. Then we jumped on the trampoline. We also talked to her parents and then I went home and slept.

My Way Home

On my way home I see my school it's big and brown it reminds me of my brother because he goes to summer school. Beside my school are gas stations one is green and the other is blue. I turn left and I see a lot of houses some have full green grass and others have patches of dirt. I stop by where White Castle is at. I go straight until I see Dominos and turn left. Again I see more houses only this time they all have nice grass. I go straight until I see the third stop sign and turn right. More houses and there are kids getting wet or playing basketball. I keep going straight and get to my house which has nice grass and my neighbors are playing Frisbee.

Edwin B.

My Weekend

Saturday

On Saturday we went canoeing. We went to canoe at Sugar Creek. It is almost an hour from our house. So we went to the office to rent 2 canoes. Me and my brother were in one and my little sister was with my mom and dad on the other canoe. Of course the water was warm 'cause the drought in Indiana. So we got on the boat and were on our journey of the 3 mile canoeing. It was fun cause we went under 3 bridges and saw many animals like squirrels, fishes, and other things. It was the funnest day of the week.

Sunday

It was a big day for us cause we were facing a hard team. They were really good. So we needed to be on our A game. So the game started and we already started to see frustration. Then at the end of the half it was 3-2. We were losing. So the other half started and we started to play even harder and we won the game 9-4. We beat them so bad we made them cry. So we are the undefeated team in the league.

Eric M.

Going golfing

I went golfing a long time ago. I went to a new golf place. Me and my family went there because it was fun to play somewhere else. My sister kept missing when she when she hit the ball. I laughed when my sister got mad. When I hit the golf ball I saw it going towards water. I had to go ask someone that worked there if they could give me another golf ball. I tried not to hit the golf ball hard. When me and my family finished playing golf we went inside of the golf place. There was an arcade inside. We had to get coins to play the games. When we finished playing the games we got our tickets so we could get prizes. I got a lot of prizes and my sister got a little bit of prizes, then we left.

At the Zoo

At the zoo I got to touch my favorite animal, the shark. When I touched them, they felt slimy. I touched two of them. It was too hot outside. Then me and my group went to the dolphin show. My group got to sit in front so we could get wet by the dolphins. After the dolphin show we went to go see the desert animals. When my group went in there it was hot. After lunch my group got to go to the water park and the rollercoasters.

Jesus C.

New School Start

One more month until school starts again in August for me. I'll enter 8th grade this year. It's not going to be that interesting since it's my second year there. I'll see the same teachers, principal, and things there. Hopefully this year goes fast and fun. I haven't bought my uniform or school supplies yet, but I still have plenty of time for that. My goal for this school year is to get no tardy, no absences, and no late homework. My biggest goal for me is to get straight A's all year, not only 3 or 2 times. This is also my last year in middle school, so I want to leave a perfect reputation of myself there. I'm going to try my best more this than in 7th grade. I hope this year goes out perfect as I plan it to be.

Dulce's 15

"Wow!" everything looks astonishing and very creative. I'm at Dulce's 15 party, I see Rosa dancing with Dulce. They are pretty good dancers. Trival music is playing, everyone is having a magnificent time. I approach Dulce and say, "Happy 15 birthday" and hug her. Her dress is red and gold. It looks fantastic on her. I see many familiar faces there, some of them are from LILY. Mostly everybody is wearing a dress for the girls or suit for the boys. It's so amazing seeing Dulce being happy. I wish her the best!

Jocelyn M.

Water

The water was so clear, it had a beautiful color and more because the sun was right above it and it was making the water very shiny. As the water flows, looking all cool and refreshing, every kid wants to drink it. The coldness going down your body. Kids yelling "I want some!" or "Give me some!", "It's my turn!" Waiting for their turn impatiently. Screaming, pushing, yelling, crying and fighting for you to give them some water.

Going Home

Going home is like taking a newborn baby home. Even though you can't see that the baby is happy about going home, the baby is happy and that's how I feel when I'm in the car, seatbelt on, ready to go to my cold refreshing house when my dad starts the car. I'm in a relaxed mood, the wind is my face, and "boom" my dad hits the bump going out the church. My hair on my face, the car going up and down 'cause of the bumpy roads. Giving a left turn, ready to be home. Stopping at the gas station to get a 99¢ Arizona Half & Half—ice tea & lemonade. The coldness going down your throat.

Nancy M.

Zoo Avengers

On Friday, June 22, 2012 the LILY students and staff went to the Indianapolis Zoo. When we got to the zoo we were separated into groups. My group and another group got together because it wasn't many of us. When we got in our groups we got a paper for a scavenger hunt in the zoo. All of the groups started at the Dolphin show. We sat in the splash zone. One of the scavenger hunt missions was to "Dougie with the Dolphins" one of the teachers danced and so did some students. The dolphin show was so cool, they waved at us and did flips and got us wet when they landed. Everyone was happy and ready to start the fun trip ahead.

When the dolphin show finished we headed to "The Desert." We had two missions for the scavenger hunt in the desert. First we had to hide with the turtles and then we had to slither with the snakes. Every mission we accomplished, we had to take a picture doing it. After about thirty minutes of Walking we had to walk ALL the way back to the front so we could eat lunch. Some people in my group didn't like the lunch that LILY had brought, so we went to the Zoo Cafe to buy some pizza because we didn't want to have empty stomachs. There were some really long lines so we stretched our lunch time to an hour instead of just thirty minutes. We finished eating and took a look at our scavenger hunt list, by lunch we already had done the simple ones, like, take a picture with a zookeeper and spell LILY next to the flower garden.

After lunch we went to see the rest of the zoo animals. The more we walked the hotter it got. We saw baby giraffes, buffaloes, zebras, and ostriches. We had done almost all of the missions on the scavenger hunt list. The more we walked the hotter it got. We stopped at the splash park. We were there for a bout five minutes and then we had to leave so we could finish the rest of the tour. We dried off a bit and headed to the Aquarium. The last few on the list were missions in the aquarium. My favorites were pet the sharks and wobble with the penguins. Our very last was, shiver with the polar bears. After that we headed to the entrance, half dry, and ran to the buses. I don't know about everyone else but I had a great time!

Nuri R.

Boy in the Back

I remember the silent boy in the back of the room. His sweet smile that escaped from hiding rarely. The intelligent eyes that shyly flickered from face to face. The soft and gentle voice spoke only when it was necessary, but never if it was not needed. His dark brown skin that seemed always to be one solid and rich tone. A calm and down to earth demeanor that never changed, though he usually kept to himself. His simple wardrobe that showed that looks didn't mean a lot to him. The way his whole face and body animated when a soccer ball would roll his way or the chance to show off his skills surfaced. The way he was totally oblivious to the multitude of girls that hit on him or left not so subtle hints about the way they felt about him.

Community: Marching Band

Buckets of sweat pour off of determined and proud kids. Instruments glistening in the hot sun as the director guides us on the blacktop. Band members guzzling down water to stay hydrated as often as they can. Different notes, beats, and speeds all forming together to create the perfect melody in the repetitive practice song. Drum majors clapping in time to show us how fast we should be marching. "One, two, three, four, five, six, lock push!" yelled over the speaker.

Rosa M.

You

I had said I didn't want to see, didn't want to talk with you, thing is that every second that goes by without havin' you say, 'Hi' or ask how

I've been has me so frustrated...you made smile, made laugh. Sometimes even made me feel like I wasn't just someone else...oh my God, I cry to myself, cry tears that are invisible to everyone else and I try to not make myself look weak...but YOU, you had to go away and it gave me pain and now I don't even feel like wakin' up because I dream, I dream of our good times full of laughter and clear blue skies...I'm afraid of opening my eyes, I'm afraid because if I do so, I'll have to face reality, I have to face that fact that you're not here with me...I actually believe that when it rains, it's just God cryin' with me, so I won't feel alone and all I do is think about makin' the day go faster...YOU have made me feel what it's like to be a beautiful flower, a beautiful flower dyin' for water and I realize time has gone by and I'm finished...the harsh times I have tried to forget these past few days, but in my heart they'll stay because of all the damage and to know that I can sit and remember when it used to be just you and me, walkin' with our heads held high and showin' our pride...always knowin' that as my own little angel I could always see the magical world, the magical world where I could go every time I felt bad and you'd be there waitin' for me with a smile...many people may call you 'imaginary friend' but I call you friend because that's what you are—a friend...I can close my eyes and see the tall pretty green grass and big fat trees that always look young—just full of life and their branches long enough to make a strong swing...with no real problem I climbed to the

top and look at you and say that I never want
to leave.

Salvador R.
School Soccer Team
This past spring I graduated from my middle
school. Harshman Magnet Middle School is the
best middle school I've been to. The best thing
about it was my soccer team. The soccer team
was like my second family because we talk to
each other when we need it. I treat all of them
like my brothers. The coach is an awesome
coach because he acts like a teenager, but
during the games we focus. This upcoming fall
I am joining my high school soccer team which
will be coached by our middle school coach. I
plan on having a great season this fall. One of
our rivals is George Washington Community
High School. We have had some wins and they
have had some wins. This fall we will beat
them.

Weekend Plans
Well, Saturday my mom and a bunch of my
cousins are going to help her cook the food
because there will be a lot of people at my little
brother's birthday party. One thing for sure, I
know my mom is making her rice with mole.
The rice is steaming and hot and has a radish
with orange color. It will be added with the
mole with chicken. The mole is hot with a
brown color and has one of a kind taste,
especially with the chicken. My mom also

makes her own salsa verde or salsa rojo. They are both different because of their color. They both have different taste. The salsa verde is made with green tomato and green chili. And then adds some onion.

Saint Florian

Author Index

Hope L.	33
Imari Q.	35
Isaiah D.	35
Jaden P.	36
Jaelyn W.	37
Jaime J.	38
Jalen K.	39
Janai S.	40
Jimmesia J.	40
Jordan J.	42
Jordan Q.	42
Jordan T.	43
Joshua P.	44
Josiah H.	44
Kaleb M.	45
Kennedi A.	46
Lauren H.	47
Lucas Y.	48
Lyrik E.	49
Maiya D.	50
Mar'Kayla K.	50
Marquia T.	51
Montgomery B.	53
Morgan Wi.	54
Morgan Wr.	55
Nakil S.	55
Nehemiah A.	55
Nia D.	56
Noah H.	56
Rafael S.	57
Roderick W.	58
Roman D.	58
Roy B.	59
Shania B.	59
Shawn F.	60

Concord

La Plaza